Published by: TAG Books
P.O. Box 111
Independence OR 97351

Distributed by: Wade Martin's Bonanza Distribution
Bend, OR 97701

Cover Design and Artwork by Sheila Somerville

Printed in the United States

Second Edition

Copyright 1993 - Gary D. Trump

ISBN: 0-9622856-0-9

Other books in the Uncle Bud series:

I Remember When

Martha and I made an agreement when we got married: I'd make all the major decisions and she'd make all the minor ones. I outsmarted her on that deal. We've been married thirty-five years, and there hasn't been one major decision to make.

When the kids were little, Martha told me she wanted me to build a playpen six feet square.

"Oh," I said, "you want something they can run around in and not get out."

"No," she sighed, "I just want to be someplace where they can't get in."

I gave my citizenship some exercise by going to vote the other day. As usual, I had the place pretty much to myself. It was a regular hotbed of voter apathy. I guess I can understand it though. Still, people should get out and vote. After all, politicians may never see the light — but they do feel the heat.

When I was a kid, there was an old buckaroo named Sam Johnson who worked for different ranches in the area. Sam loved to tell stories, and he liked to tell 'em to a tenderfoot or a kid. He'd tell the story, and it would keep getting a little more unbelievable all the time until the victim caught on. Once, in a cow camp in the Blues, old

1

Sam and I were sitting around the fire one evening and Sam started talking about his younger days.

"Yuh know," Sam started out, "when I was a kid, we had some stuff made out of rubber, like ground sheets, to keep you dry when you slept out. Buggies and light wagons had hard rubber tires. Oh, you could find several things around made out of rubber, but then they went to makin' all kinds of stuff out of it. Our hired hand bought himself a pair of rubber boots. He shook his head slowly. "They was mighty strange."

"What's so strange about a pair of rubber boots?" I asked.

"That India rubber we had back then was different than it is now. It was either real hard or real soft. I tried on them boots. They was awful springy to walk around in and, in the end, they killed the fella who owned 'em."

"How did they do that?" I asked with my fool mouth hanging open.

"Well," said Sam, "we had us a hard windstorm one night, and it tore some shingles off the barn roof and loosened some others. It was a big ol' barn, about three stories tall, and Pa sent the hired man up there to patch the roof. He wore his new rubber boots so he wouldn't slip."

Sam poured himself a cup of coffee and sat back, staring into the flames. "It was a shock to all of us," he said sadly.

"What was?" I asked, mentally kicking myself for playing into his hands.

"That hired hand was right at the peak of the roof," Sam said quietly. "I guess he got over-confident 'cause he was walkin' around up there like he owned the world. He walked right to the edge, and his last step was on a loose shingle. It flew out from under him, and he came down off that roof like a ton of brick."

"The fall killed him?"

"In a way it did," Sam went on. "He turned over two or three times in the air and lit feet first. Like I said, he had those India rubber boots on and when he hit, he bounced. We was all amazed, but thankful that it looked like he'd come out all right. Sam shook his head. "He bounced alright, but he bounced real high ... clear up past the barn roof. Ever' time he hit, he bounced a little higher. We just sat there and watched him. We was plumb dumbfounded, I'm tellin' you. By noon he was only comin' down ever' five minutes or so, and by six o'clock his landin's was ten or fifteen minutes apart. We done ever'thing we could think of to save him. Along there toward the end, we noticed that his ears looked froze and the buzzards had been roostin' on him. We figgered it could go on that way for days an' days."

"So what did you do?" I asked, knowing I'd been had once again.

"It was for the best." Sam sniffed and dabbed at his eyes. "It was a kindness really. We had to shoot him to keep him from starvin' to death."

3

You can never tell about tourists. One walked in here the other day and asked "How much for a hamburger?".

"$3.00."

"How much for a hamburger and fries?"

"We call that a 'hamburger special.' It's $3.95."

"$3.95?"

"Yeah, but don't forget, with the hamburger special you get free fries."

And then he walked out. Go figure.

Modern medicine does some wonderful things. Still, more often than not, a doctor's main job is to keep from screwing things up too bad until nature can take care of the problem.

Martha doesn't have a sense of humor. She says women have to be that way or they would never fall in love with men. They'd be too busy laughing at them.

I've been getting these letters in the mail lately telling me I'm a finalist in some contest. It's hard to get excited about it when the upper right corner of the envelope says "bulk rate."

Banana peel rubbed on a mosquito bite will take away the itch.

Not long before my Dad died, he got to talking about the tough times people went through during the Depression. There was very little money in circulation and practically no work available. A lot of times people traded goods and services for their needs.

"I got a job one fall workin' for a potato farmer," Dad said. "There wasn't any machinery like they have now. They just plowed up the spuds and picked 'em up by hand. The farmer was like everybody else ... he didn't have any cash money. We took our pay in sacks of potatoes.

"When the job was done, we loaded our sacks on a truck, and the farmer hauled us to town. I went to trading around, and by the time I was done, I had a pair of shoes, some new clothes, and three dollars in cash. Then I started to look for another job.

"I was standing on the street talking to a man about a job he'd heard about when this young fella about my age came up to us.

'*Excuse me,*' he said.

"I looked over at him and saw he was pretty thin. His clothes had patches on the patches and his shoes were worn out, but he was clean and so was everything he wore.

'*Yeah?*' The guy I'd been talkin' to said.

'*Would either of you gentlemen like to buy a safety razor? It's a good one.*'

'*No,*' said the fella I'd been talkin' to as he turned back toward me.

"Well, I'd been watchin' all this, and over this young man's shoulder I saw a young woman standing about twenty feet away. She was like her husband, rail thin and her worn out dress was patched, but freshly washed. Two little kids, a boy and a girl, and dressed in clean, tattered clothes clung to their mother's dress. That young wife was carryin' a baby in her arms that couldn't have been over a month old.

"The fella I'd been talkin' with was sayin' something, but I held up my hand to stop him and looked at the young man. *'You're sellin' a safety razor?'*

'It's a good one.' He dug it out of his shirt pocket and tried to hand it to me.

"I've already got a razor," I said, pushin' it away.

'Twenty-five cents,' he said, and you could tell he was desperate.

'Why?'

'The baby has to have milk. Couldn't you buy it mister?' He swallowed hard and held out the razor again. *'Please?'*

"I don't need a razor, I said, "but I've got three dollars. I'll split it with you."

Dad told me this story while we were sitting in the kitchen of the old house having a cup of coffee. In all my life I'd never heard him mention this incident before.

"Sometimes," Dad said, "I wonder how they made out."

So do I. And I wonder if I would have the courage to give half of what I had to a stranger in need when I hadn't the slightest idea where my next dollar was coming from. I wonder about

6

something else, too. I wonder how anyone could live fifty years of his life and not think to mention something like that to anyone, not even his son. I guess if there's a difference between people then and now, it has something to do with that attitude.

Doing the right thing was the rule, not the exception, and people didn't expect praise or rewards for doing what they should.

You can use ice on gum or candle wax in your carpet. Once it's hard, you can pick it off a lot easier.

Martha and I ran into the Bennets at the art festival a while back. We came to a display of modern art, and Tom stood there looking at one painting for quite a while. He was twisting his head one way and another trying to figure it out. Finally he looked over at me and said "what's this thing supposed to be, anyhow?"

I looked at the card under the picture. "It says 'Antelope At Sunrise.'"

"Then why ain't it?" growled Tom, as he walked away.

With the high rate of divorce these days, I think I've finally hit on a way to get rich. There must be a real need out there for a wash and wear wedding dress.

Tom claims he was out visiting Luther at his farm a while back and noticed he had a pig with a wooden leg. When Tom asked him about it, Luther started telling him what a wonderful animal that pig was.

"I had a conveyor belt runnin' to the feed chopper," Luther said, "and I hit my head on a beam. Fell right onto the belt, stunned senseless. Quick as a flash that critter ran over and pulled me off that belt. Saved my life."

"That's really something," Tom said.

"Not only that," Luther went on, "but once the house caught on fire in the middle of the night. That critter smelled smoke and went to squealin' an' raisin' a ruckus. Woke me up. Saved my life."

"That's just amazing," Tom said. "But you know, Luther, that still doesn't explain the wooden leg."

Luther kind of puffed up and looked at Tom like he was simple. "Well!" he said. "A good hog like that, you don't think I'd eat him all at once do ya?"

Luther sat right there while Tom told that story. He just nodded and agreed with it and never cracked a smile. Well, I wouldn't call either of them liars, but it's a known fact that when either of them wants to call his dog, he has to hire somebody to do it for him.

8

It seems like civilization has pretty much reached all the people of the world. Well, all those who have anything we want anyhow.

Americans seem to think the answer to any problem is to throw money at it. Well, the schools need more money. The government needs more money. The charities need more money. If this was a baseball game, we'd be the only team with more catchers than pitchers.

I'm really showing my age with this one, but I have to tell you one of my earliest memories is of mom's old wood range. It stood a foot or so off the floor on its heavy iron legs, and that space underneath was the perfect hideout for a little boy. Oh, sure, there might be a dust bunny or two under there, but what little boy was ever afraid of dust or dirt?

On those cold winter days when the mercury in the thermometer shrank down to thirty below, it was the perfect spot. The linoleum would be warm from the heat of the stove, and there was often the yeasty smell of fresh bread dough rising from up in the warming oven. I can still recall my disappointment when I got too big to slide under the stove.

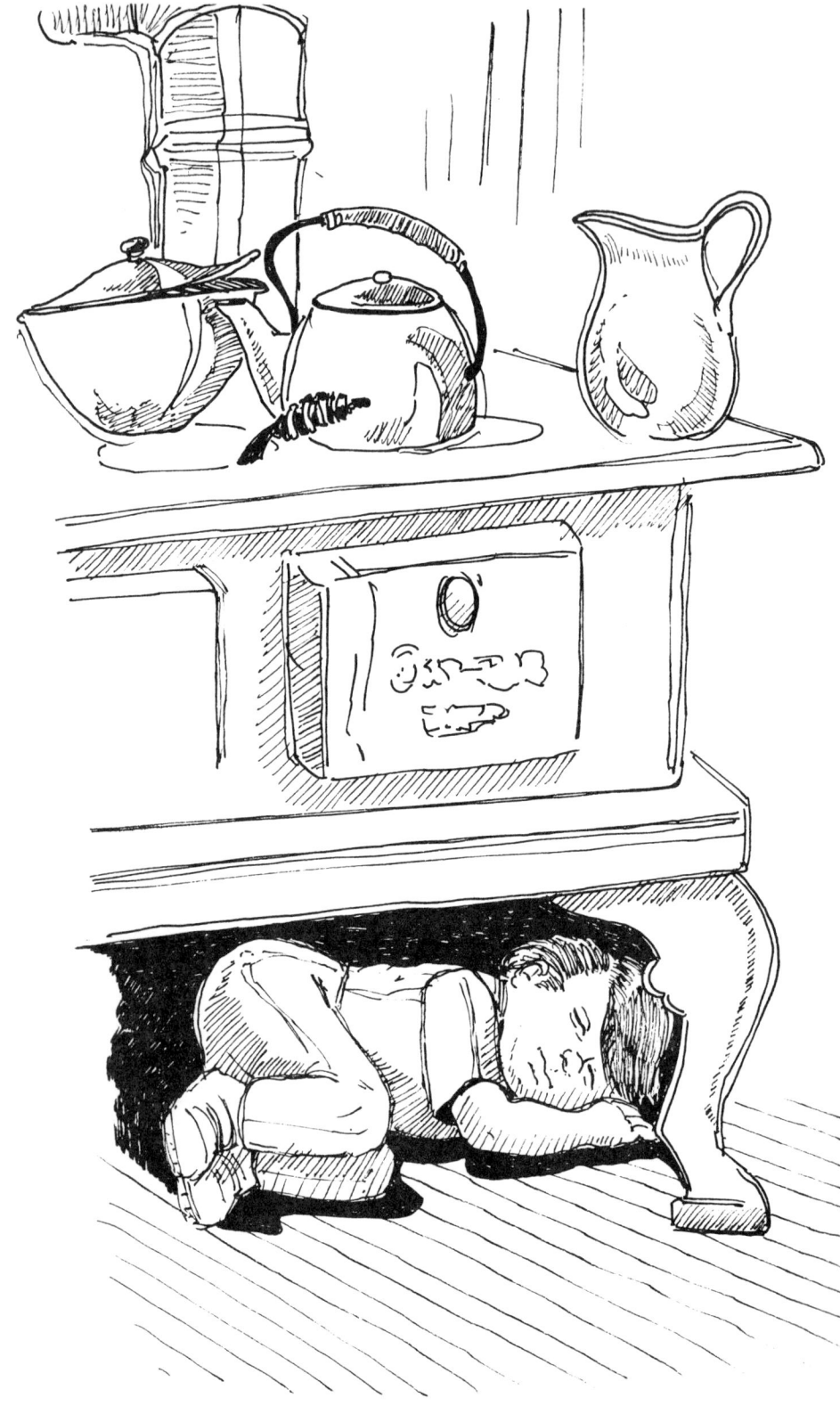

The kitchen table and the old wood range was the center of our world. The stove heated a brick for each of us on cold winter nights. We'd wrap it in a towel and take it upstairs to warm our cold feet in our cold beds. When we woke in the morning, the frost might be half an inch thick on the inside of the window. We'd jump out of bed, grab our clothes, and rush downstairs to dress by the welcome warmth of the old range.

There was a water reservoir in the back, and it provided hot water for baths. Every Saturday night out came the tin washtub, and we got a bath whether we needed it or not. Looking back, I can't remember a time when we didn't need it, but we always thought it was not only unnecessary but quite an imposition to boot.

There is still a company or two that manufactures the same old cast iron wood ranges just like the old days. I'm glad they do. Just knowing those old stoves are still out there somewhere makes me feel a little better.

While we're on the subject of wood stoves, it sure seems as if a lot more people are heating with wood these days. Well, wood is still fairly cheap, and wood heat just seems to penetrate more somehow. I've heated with wood all my life.

The big problem with wood is the risk of flue fires. I make sure I clean my chimney every year, and at least once a week, I wad up some newspaper, light it, and push it up into the stove pipe. If you keep that soot and creosote burned out, you won't have problems. Another thing I do to keep down the soot buildup is throw salt on the fire every couple of days.

It's getting harder to find now, but copper (II) sulfate works really well in keeping your chimney clean. Quite often it's the principle ingredient in the commercial soot remover that you buy in the store. Sometimes, you can buy it in bulk at a hardware or feed store. It's blue in color and is usually in granule form. Sprinkle a small handful on the fire every two or three days to keep things clean. Remember, though, that nothing can take the place of giving that flue a good brushing every fall.

Copper (II) sulfate has other uses, too. If you have tree roots growing into your sewer line, drop the granules into your toilet tank. Add enough so that when they dissolve the water is a medium blue color. If you do this on a regular basis over the summer, it will kill the tree roots back and keep your line clear.

If you have a roof with wooden shingles, you may also have a problem with moss. Copper (II) sulfate sprinkled on the roof will get rid of it. I don't know how the sulfate would affect composition shingles. I'd ask someone who knows before I'd use it on them.

Not long after they opened the golf course, Luther was in one morning as usual having a cup of coffee. "Y'know," he said, leaning both elbows on the counter, "I was out huntin' yesterday, and I got onto that golf course by mistake. I came out of a patch of brush, and there's this fat guy with a golf club tryin' to hit a ball. He's thrashin' around like he's killin' snakes, and I got so interested in watchin' him, I forgot I wasn't s'posed to be there. After a while, the guy looks up and sees me. *'Here now,'* he yells. *'What are you doin' here? This is a private club for golfers only.'* Well, I took a chaw and looked him over a while, and then I said *'Well, it looks to me like we're both trespassin.'* He got all frothy about it and left."

"They don't just play golf there," I said. "They've got tennis courts outside the clubhouse."

"I found out that very thing," Luther replied. "What that feller said made me curious, so as soon as I got home, I got in my pickup and drove over there."

Now Luther's old pickup looks like the "AFTER" picture in a seatbelt commercial, so he probably didn't make a real favorable impression on those folks when he drove in to the club. On the other hand, when he drives down the street, nobody is too anxious to split hairs about who has the right-of-way. Luther is used to driving wherever he damn well pleases. He'll park that old beater between two limousines, reach outside to open the door (the inside door latch quit working years ago), climb out, and walk away, knowing he's as good as anybody and better than some.

"I drove in there," Luther went on, "and parked. You'd think those people had never seen bib overalls before. Well, I noticed a couple fellers playin' tennis, so I strolled over to watch."

He shook his head as I refilled his cup. "I can't make head ner tail of it," he said. "Football and basketball I can understand. The cheerleaders are always yellin' 'get that ball, get that ball.' But tennis is just the opposite. They play like the ball has somethin' nasty on it. Nobody wants it. One feller hits it over that little fence, but the other feller, he don't want it neither, so he hits it right back. After a while, though, somebody gets stuck with it. Then they start talkin' about 'love' this and 'love' that, and all the while they're runnin' around in their underwear. There's somethin' kinda strange about it if you ask me."

I've got my little business here and I don't compete with anybody except myself. For one thing it makes me feel a lot more comfortable. For another, it drives some of those people with similar businesses right up the wall. No one can compete with you if you won't play the game.

14

Around a restaurant you always have to be concerned about grease fires. Baking powder makes a good dry fire extinguisher. So does three pounds of sand to one pound of baking soda — well mixed. I keep some at home, in both the kitchen and the garage.

Tom says he had a problem with a neighbor's dogs a few years back. It seems the neighbor had three big ol' dogs that liked to use Tom's yard as their personal bathroom. The neighbor kept them in during the day, but turned them loose after dark.

"I kept the backyard light on and quite often I'd see them jump the fence," Tom said. "A couple of times I went out to run 'em off and stepped in a dog pile gettin' the job done. Complaining to the neighbor didn't help. He'd just wait until I turned off the lights and went to bed. The flower beds and vegetable garden looked like they'd been attacked by giant gophers. Finally I had enough.

"Now, if I've got a dog," Tom said, "then what he drops on the ground is mine, too, and I'll scoop it up and dispose of it. I got to thinking that I'd treated my neighbor all wrong. After all, if he'd left his rake or his hoe in my yard, I'd return it to him. So I brought a couple of five gallon buckets home from the store and went to collecting dog piles. When the buckets were full, I just took them over and dumped them on his front step. I didn't know where he'd want 'em, and the buckets were mine, after all."

Tom tugged at his chin and gave a long sigh. "People are funny," he said. "That fella didn't seem to appreciate me returning his property to him. A few days later he put up a high fence, and the dogs didn't come by at all anymore."

Martha and I went to a nice restaurant awhile back. The place had half a dozen waiters. It took about an hour to get something to eat, and while I was sitting there, I got to thinking about it. They need to call those people something else. After all, who's doing all the waiting, anyhow?

Joe Endicott's dad was a livestock trader, mostly. I say "mostly" because he'd trade anything, cars to real estate, that he happened to come in possession of - and that's why the Endicotts never stayed in one place too long. They never went too far, but they were always on the move.

"My dad traded for a place in town, one time," Joe smiled. Our next door neighbor, a man named Hasker, kept chickens. Now, keepin' chickens was no big deal. Half the people in town did that and some kept a cow, too. Remember, it was a real small town then and times were tough.

"Hasker had a board fence about eight feet tall built right on his property line. It turned out to be his chicken yard. But Hasker was kind of a lazy fella. He didn't keep those chickens' wing feathers clipped, and they flew in and out of that chicken yard whenever they took a notion, which was pretty often.

"We had a shed on our place, and dad bein' a trader, it was full of stuff that kind of came and went. One thing we always had, though, were saddles and harness. Dad owned some pasture land just out of town where he kept his livestock.

"Hasker's chickens took to roostin' in our shed." Joe shook his head and sipped at his coffee. "We could have fixed it so they couldn't get in, but dad wouldn't do it. He thought it was Hasker's job to keep his chickens where they belonged. Besides, some of the other neighbors had complained about Hasker's chickens, too.

"Dad went over there three or four times and told Hasker that there was chicken manure all over his saddles and harness and whatnot. Hasker said it wasn't his problem. As far as he was concerned it was up to the other people to keep his chickens out.

"About a month later one of the neighbors happened to stop by to see Hasker one day, and he found him out back. He was catchin' his chickens and clippin' their wings.

"*Gonna keep 'em from flyin' out of the chicken yard, huh?*" the neighbor says.

"*Yeah,*" growls Hasker, "*I've got to. I've had quite a few chickens come up missin' lately.*

"*Oh, how's that?*

"*Well,*" says Hasker, and he turns to look at the board fence and our house beyond it, "*I don't want to point fingers, but every time a chicken comes up missin', I smell feathers burnin' over at Endicott's.*" With a sly smile Joe looked around at each of us. "Y'know," he said, "chickens are like watermelons. They taste better when they belong to somebody else."

Kids learn from their parents, but the opposite is true as well. The word 'patience' comes to mind.

Well, I bought this cafe, and I get up at four o'clock every morning so I can open at six. Martha tells me it's just as well. She claims I've been so damned ornery all my life that my conscience probably wouldn't let me sleep late anyway.

There's an engineer with the railroad who stops by once in a while for a hamburger and coffee. He grew up around here, and he used to spend his summers fishing down there on the river where the railroad track runs alongside. He says he used to sit there with a can of worms and a willow pole and watch the trains go by. The engineers would wave to him, and he'd wave back and dream of

running one of those big locomotives someday. Well now, he'll be bringing a train down that stretch of track in the summer, and he'll see some kid down there fishing. He'll wave and the kid will wave back. "You know," he'll say, "I'd give anything to just shut 'er down, climb out of the cab and go cut myself a willow pole. I'd sit down next to that kid and fish a while."

I've been married to Martha for thirty-five years, and I've come to the conclusion that the words 'fashionable' and 'comfortable' are exact opposites.

Ol' Elmer sometimes stops by real early for a cup of coffee after an all night session with his spiritual advisor. That's a bartender to you and me. A few years ago Elmer was ready to settle down with a woman who told him she had never tasted liquor. He said he had her convinced that he only took a little nip now and then, and when he did, he drank only the best twelve-year old scotch.

They were eating here at the cafe when she excused herself to go to the restroom. As a joke, he pulled out a flask and poured a shot into her empty coffee cup. When she got back, she noticed it right off. She picked up the cup, sniffed at the booze, and then knocked it back like a pro.

"Elmer," she said, "the wedding is off. I

won't marry a man who can't tell the difference between expensive scotch and cheap bourbon."

In college a person's intelligence and ability is often judged by the number of syllables in the words they use.

On New Year's Eve I gave each of the waitresses a bottle of champagne. A few days later I asked one of them, Jean, how she liked it. "Just right," she said.

"Just right?"

"Yeah. Any better and you'd have kept it. Any worse and nobody could drink it."

Well, I read in the paper the other day where the results of a new study revealed something else that causes cancer. Another study turned up a new factor in the incidence of heart disease. I think I'm beginning to get a handle on this. It's the same kind of theory that the puritans must have had. In other words, if it tastes good or feels good, then it must be sinful and therefore bad for you.

Of course, the government funds the majority of these studies, and I'm thrilled that they would go to all that trouble just to keep their taxpayers alive a little longer. The media is sure to make the results known and, since I'm a good American, I believe everything the media tells me.

On the other hand, a more cynical person might get the idea that if these studies didn't come up with something, then the funding would stop and a bunch of scientists would be out looking for work. But I'd never think anything like that. Not me.

Tom claims he isn't bald. He argues he only has a real high forehead. Once, when the kids were teenagers, they gave him a billfold for Christmas. Considering what Christmas costs anymore, he says they may as well have given him hair oil.

Tom's barber makes a good profit on him, since there's so little wear and tear on the equipment. The barber has an old dog that lays around the shop all day. The dog took to doing that when he found out his master whacks off a chunk of ear now and then. Tom says he'd change barbers, but then they'd probably both go hungry.

I may as well tell you up front that while I do know all the latest questions — I'm not too sure about the answers.

For cleaning oven grates and barbecue grills, try putting them in a garbage bag and then spraying them with oven cleaner. Do it outside if you can, because the fumes are dangerous to breathe. Tie the bag tight and leave it overnight. The next day take the grate or grill from the bag and swish it off with the hose.

Grills are easier to clean if you spray them with one of these non-stick cooking sprays before you use them.

I don't know if you were ever taken to the woodshed as a kid, but if you were, then you're a member of a not-to-exclusive group. Parents back then all had their preferred tools for the job. Mom might use a spatula (now you can guess how the spat-u-la got its name) or a hairbrush. Dad might use his belt. My dad liked a razor strop. For those of you who don't know, that's the long piece of leather used to hone straight razors.

Well, maybe you've been taken to the woodshed a few times, and no doubt it seemed like a long trip, but there are those of us who belong to a more elite group.

Now, I've been around some and seen the elephant in places like Hong Kong, New York and London, but they weren't long trips. My dear ol' dad used to take me to the woodshed and then send me back to the house for the razor strop. He'd sit there on the chopping block and roll a cigarette while I made the journey. Not only was that the world's longest trip, but my lovin' parent didn't like to be kept waiting and tended to get a little testy when I took too long. It's odd how motivation and the lack of it can pull both ways sometimes.

I've heard it said that what colleges really teach students is how to work for somebody else. Makes you kind of wonder who all those college graduates are working for.

There was a young fella that used to come in here every morning for breakfast. He'd pull up in a new car and come strutting in here like he owned the world. He had an attitude alright. One morning Tom, Pete, Luther and Joe were here having coffee as usual when the kid made some sarcastic crack about "old pensioners."

"Y'know," Luther said to nobody in particular, "it must be real painful to have a head that's swelled so far out of shape."

"It ain't the swelling that's painful," put in Joe, "but it hurts like blazes when it starts to shrink back to normal size."

Haven't seen the kid since.

Almost any night on television you can see the latest protest. There's a crowd of people carrying signs wanting this done or that banned or whatever. Generally, they're well meaning folks with a sprinkling of lunatics here and there. These people really believe in what they're doing. They donate their time, effort and cash to the cause.

The more radical ones wait until the television crew gets there before they pick out a cop to cuss, kick, and spit on. Then the cameras can show them being hauled off to the pokey. It's good publicity and generates contributions from like-minded citizens.

As I've said before, I'm not a cynic. I look on in innocent wonder at these dedicated individuals. Not once do I think that somewhere in the background, giggling and counting the cash, are the founders of some of these groups - whose motives are less than pure. I would never think such things.

There are professional athletes and there are college athletes. One group is paid by check. The other isn't.

You know some games are named so you can tell a little bit about them. Baseball, football, racketball, all give you an idea what to expect. I got to thinking about golf, and I'll bet the fella that invented it probably gave it a descriptive name, too. But then nobody would play the game, so he had to disguise what golf was all about. That's when he spelled it backwards.

Marnie was just sixteen when we met, and I was a couple years older. Her mother had come to the valley to work in the canneries, and Marnie attended my old high school. She made a few casual friends there, but not many. Marnie was so quiet and withdrawn that not many people would notice she was around.

We dated that one summer, and I learned more about her. She was an only child and didn't remember her father. Marnie's mom had no skills and so they moved a lot, looking for steady work. Marnie was fun to be around once you got to know her. With a ready laugh and sparkle in her eye, she opened up to friends and let them see who she really was.

Marnie wasn't beautiful, but she certainly wasn't homely either. She was of average height, thin, and graceful in her walk and movements. Of all the people I have known, she was, I think, the most gentle and considerate of others. I never knew her to intentionally cause discomfort to anyone.

I had things to do, places to go, and people to see, so there wasn't time to hang around where I was. A year later I was in the Army, and a year after that I was fighting for my life in a steamy, god-forsaken jungle half a world away. I lost track of Marnie.

But then a friend wrote that Marnie had diabetes, and she was having a hard time. I meant to drop her a line, maybe cheer her up. I should have; I didn't.

When I came home on leave, I heard that Marnie and her mom had moved to a town a couple hundred miles away. That had been six months before I got back. Three months after that her mother was killed in a car accident with a drunk driver. I meant to drive up and see Marnie, but there were so many people to see and so many things to do that I just never got around to it.

I was finishing out my enlistment when another letter told me Marnie had gotten married. She married a young man named Kenny, and I remembered him well. Kenny's parents were dead, and he was raised by his grandmother. Well, it was just Marnie and Kenny alone now, and I wished them well. I was going to send them a card or a gift, but I would be getting out of the service in a month. I promised myself I'd go and see them as soon as I got home.

College turned out to be a lot tougher than I thought. It took up all my time, and I still hadn't managed to drive the two hundred miles to see Marnie and Kenny. It was just before spring break when I heard they'd had a baby. It was a little girl and they'd named her Tiffany. I wanted to get up and see them, but I was running low on money, so during spring break I went to work for a local rancher on spring roundup. He liked my work and wanted me back just as soon as school let out for the summer. I agreed.

It was the next spring when I heard about the car wreck. It was another drunk driver. Kenny and Tiffany were killed on impact, but Marnie's

injuries were not serious. It happened during finals week. I couldn't get away.

It was a couple of weeks later when a friend called me and said Marnie wasn't getting better. In fact, she was worse. Classes had just started and I wanted to finish out the week, but then I'd drive up to see her. I thought maybe her diabetes was causing problems with her recovery. Well, I suppose it was a problem, but it certainly wasn't the only one.

When I got to the hospital, the nurse asked if I was a relative. I told her, no, that Marnie had no relatives that I knew of. The nurse told me only two people had been to see her, and they weren't relatives either. She needed to find someone who could make a decision since Marnie could no longer make them for herself.

"What's wrong?" I asked, as a cold chill passed over me.

"Her injuries aren't that serious," the nurse said quietly, "but she just decided to quit living. You didn't know she was in a coma?"

"No," I whispered, "I didn't."

They let me see her, and I sat beside the bed and held her hand a while. I talked to her a little bit, and then I kissed her on the forehead and I left. It was a long drive home.

There were only three people at the funeral, and I knew the other two. Patty got married that same year and moved to the east coast. Mike died three years later in a logging accident.

It's been a long time, and I still live two hundred miles away, but I passed by the cemetery a couple of years ago. I stopped in at a market and bought cleaning supplies before I drove onto the grounds. I must have looked for an hour before I found the gravesite. The headstones needed cleaning, so I brushed away the grass clippings and went to work. The graves shouldn't have been hard to find. They're off by themselves over by the fence, not far from the tall sycamore that was only a seedling at the time. Marnie is there with her little family, and they're together ... alone.

Of the ghosts that come in the night to sit on the foot of my bed, Marnie is the most quiet. Of the spirits that ask "Why did you do what you did?" or "Why didn't you do what you should?" ... hers is the most gentle. In the stillness of the night I feel sorrow not only for her but for the man I might have been ... and I thank her for her kindness.

After having dinner out with friends, I've noticed that the conversation often has an effect on my digestion. For example: "Put your money away, Bud. This is my treat." Or "Gee, I guess I must have left my wallet at home."

It's nice to go do your duty and vote. You can walk away knowing that because of people like yourself at least half of those turkeys won't be elected.

I used to think it was nice to see a family come in, order a meal, and say grace before they ate. Then I heard that the custom of saying grace goes clear back to the days of the nomadic hunters and gatherers. It seems that, since they moved around a lot, they often came across strange things that they thought might be good to eat, but weren't too sure. They took to asking their gods to bless the food so they wouldn't be poisoned. Now a family comes in, orders a meal, says grace, and I have to wonder ...

We've got a storage shed not far from the house, and a skunk decided to establish his homestead there not long ago. The shed is on a cement block foundation, and there's about a foot of clearance between the floor and the ground. When he moved in, it was pretty obvious that somebody would have to move out. It's not that I'm anti-social either. If I was, I'd be wearing the same kind of cologne my new neighbor favored. It kind of makes you wonder how romance ever manages to blossom in the skunk world. It looks (smells) like they would have all died out after one generation. I don't know if it's true, but I've heard that a grizzly bear will yield the right-of-way to nobody but a skunk.

Well, I went to the store and bought some mothballs. There was an opening in the foundation of the shed where the skunk was going in and out. I tossed a handful of mothballs as far back under there as I could. Within twenty-four hours, our new neighbor had packed up and left. They don't like the smell of mothballs. Personally, I don't see how they can smell anything, but it works.

Now that I think about it, I'm not sure I should have mentioned that part about grizzlies giving skunks a wide berth. I can just see it now. Somebody is going to hear about this, put two and two together, get five and a half and say, "Aha! This means I can go hunting grizzly bears with a pocketful of mothballs and a slingshot."

You don't think it will happen? Listen, one of these days you'll be watching one of those nature shows on television, and you'll see a grizzly amblin' down a trail and pausing occasionally to spit out a mothball or two. Count on it.

Elmer's dad had been a prohibition agent. It seems he knew of this one family that he strongly suspected of making moonshine. They lived a way out in the sticks up near the head of a canyon. One day Elmer's dad drove up there. When he pulled into the yard, he didn't see anybody but a raggedly little kid about ten years old, who looked like he didn't know the meaning of the word "bath."

Elmer's dad got out of the car. "Hi, sonny. Where's everybody at?"

"They're all workin' up at the still," the kid says, waving his arm at the timbered slope behind him.

Oh, I've got 'em now, Elmer's dad thinks to himself. *Now, all I've gotta do is find 'em in all that brush.*

He sidles up to the kid. "Say, sonny, if you'll take me up there to the still, I'll give you fifty cents when we get back."

"Okay," says the kid, "but give me the money now."

"Why?"

"Mister, you ain't comin' back."

"You know," says Pete, "dealin' with politicians is kinda like shearin' pigs. There's a whole lot of wigglin' and squealin', but damn little wool."

As far as boots are concerned, I think the Army figures it this way: Look at a cow — she's got four feet per cowhide. A soldier only has two feet, so he gets half a cowhide. To say that those boots they gave me were too big would be an understatement. The day I took 'em off for the last time, there were parts of them that were still unexplored territory — never set foot on by man.

I always keep a can of hand cleaner at the house. When I'm working at home and my clothes get stained or greasy, I rub a little hand cleaner into the stain before I toss my dirty clothes in the laundry hamper. If the hand cleaner isn't handy, I use cooking oil. Either way, the clothes sit there for hours or days before they're washed, and the stains usually come right out.

It's hard teaching a kid to be both tactful and truthful. Or, in other words, when to lie and when not to.

Cecil and Morton took a trip to Seattle a few years ago. I don't remember the business that took them there, but they shared a hotel room. Like Cecil and Morton are apt to do, they had a few drinks at the hotel bar. They made a few new friends and had a few more drinks and, eventually, the party moved up to their room. I think they were up on the third floor, and the party lasted long past midnight.

The next morning Morton woke up in the hospital with a cast on one arm, one leg, and bandages wrapped around him here and there. Cecil was sitting in a chair next to the bed, and Morton was, understandably, a little curious as to how he came to be there.

"What happened to me?" he asked.

"Well," said Cecil, "you broke your arm and

your leg."

"But how did it happen?"

"You got pretty drunk last night," Cecil replied. "There were all these other fellers in the room, and you got in an argument with 'em."

"What about?"

"You bet you could jump out the window, fly around the hotel and fly right back in the same window."

"My God! You didn't let me do it, did you?"

"Let you!" wailed Cecil, "I lost fifty dollars on you myself!"

Things have probably changed by now, but when I worked at the plant in town, the workers were all men. There were women in the front office, of course, but out on the floor there wasn't a woman to be found. Shipping and receiving was at the opposite end of the plant from the office, and sometimes one of the women had to walk down there to verify an invoice or something. They were usually kidded and joked with the whole way, and sometimes it got out of hand.

Even though she had a couple of grown kids, Janet was a beautiful woman. She usually was the one who had to walk down to shipping and receiving. I admired her a lot and not just because of her looks. Janet had been around the block once or twice, and no matter how hard they tried, those guys couldn't rattle her.

The worst offender of them all was Ed, in the sheet metal department. Ed and I worked together a lot, because some of the pieces we handled were pretty large. I know there were times when Janet walked by that one of his smart cracks embarrassed me, so it couldn't have been too comfortable for her.

In the summer the temperature in the plant would get pretty high. Every morning before work Ed would go into the mens' room and peel off every stitch of clothing and put on his coveralls so he could be a little cooler. That's what he'd done the day it happened.

Ed liked to smoke those little cigars and, while we were working at the metal break, he lit one up. He'd put it down on the machine when he needed to use both hands, then pick it up and take a drag before putting it down again. A foreman came by, talked a couple of minutes, and then went on his way. Before we started work again Ed looked around.

"Where's my seegar?"

"Beats me," I said.

After Ed took another quick look around, we went back to work. A couple of minutes later Ed squalled like a mashed cat and went to tearing at his coveralls. He pulled them down around his ankles. A wisp of smoke rose from the material as Ed stood in his birthday suit and examined the burn on his belly. We were both so engrossed in what had happened that neither of us heard the click of high heels until they were almost upon us.

Ed raised his head, his eyeballs bulging out to where you could have knocked them off with a stick.

Janet was walking by only three feet away. She never batted an eye. "Nice to see you too, Ed."

I worked there a couple more years, and whenever Janet walked back to shipping and receiving, the only glimpse she ever got of Ed was once when she saw him disappear around a corner.

Have you noticed that people these days seem to give some pretty weird reasons for getting a divorce? I guess it's alright though. They probably got married for some pretty weird reasons.

Joe claims that when his dad first came west, he came out alone looking for a place to move his family. There was an old Indian here in town that was pointed out as having a wonderful memory. Joe's dad walked up to him and said "What did you have for breakfast exactly twenty-five years ago today?"

The old fellow thought a while and said "Eggs."

Joe's dad just laughed and went on his way.

Joe says the family was living in the midwest then, and it took a couple years for his dad to find the right place, buy it, and go back for the wife and kids. It took another year to get things taken care of back there, so it was three or four years before the move was completed. When they got here, the first fella Joe's dad happened to see was that old Indian. As he was passing by, just to be friendly, Joe's dad said "How."

The old Indian stopped, looked at him, and then thought a minute. "Over easy," he said.

If you have central heat with floor vents, you can make the house smell better by using sheets of fabric softener. Just wad up a sheet, lift the vent, and drop it in. Make sure that the vent pipe turns at a right angle so the sheet will stay put, and you can replace it whenever you like.

Shortly after you buy your new car, you find it necessary to go to the shopping center. Not wanting scratches or nicks on your new buggy, you park clear out on the far side of the lot, a quarter mile from the stores, and at least a hundred yards from the nearest automobile. Carefully locking up, you hike all the way to the building, looking over your shoulder once or twice at your shiny new car as it sits there - alone and unblemished.

Once inside, you quickly find what you need and head for the cash registers. There are several lines with six or eight people each, but you're lucky. There is one where a lady is just completing her purchase, and there is only one guy in line. But it turns out that the guy is determined to pay by credit card. He has fourteen of them, all either expired or charged to the limit. He wants to argue with the cashier about it.

Half an hour later you're finally outside and walking toward the place you left your new car. Only you can't see your car. Where you left it you can see only a tight knot of automobiles squeezed in all around. Besides the cars, there is sure to be an old school bus with peeling blue paint manned by a gaggle of aging hippies. There will also be at least a dozen kids, each one a walking advertisement for mandatory birth control.

The bus will be parked so close to your car it would be difficult to slide a playing card between them. On the other side of your pride and joy will be either an old pickup or ancient station wagon with one side bashed in and a headlight missing. The kids, meanwhile, have torn a hunk of plywood away from where the windows used to be on the bus and are chasing each other in and out and around in a circle, which includes the hood of your car being used as a slide.

Maybe cars should come pre-dented and scratched. Think of all the grief it would save. Think of all the frustrated hippies.

Tom isn't much on camping out. "I used to be, when I was a kid," he said. Then one day I was workin' in a field a couple miles from the house,

and when I finished I walked over to the road to wait for my dad to pick me up. It was just an old gravel road and a culvert ran under it there. I sat down astraddle that culvert and waited for my dad. I was just sittin' there swingin' my legs back and forth when a skunk walked out of the culvert. Well, at the time, it seemed like too good a chance to pass up, so I just kicked him in the butt."

Tom wiped his hand across his mouth and pulled at his chin. "I had to camp out in the back yard for a month," he said with a sigh. "Took my meals on the porch and had to ride in the back of the pickup whenever we went anywhere. No, campin' ain't for me."

Martha's a big believer in budgets. Right after we were married, she sharpened her pencil and went to work. By the time she was finished, she had whittled our expenses down to where they were only about double our income.

Well, before we got married, she kept telling me that two can live as cheaply as one, and it turned out she was right. Of course, she forgot to mention that they can only eat half as much.

People who aren't happy being in their own company usually aren't happy being in mine.

When Dad decides to go fishing or hunting, he takes along enough camping gear to move the forty-niners west. If Mom decides to go along, she brings enough grub to feed 'em.

Pete had been trying to get Tom to go along on a pheasant hunting trip. "Wish you could have been with us a couple years ago," Pete said. "We drove a hundred miles south, found us a good place and got permission from the farmer to hunt and camp there. This friend of mine had a hunting dog that he said was really good, but when we got out in the field, the dog ran rabbits. He'd jump a rabbit and take off, and we wouldn't see him for an hour or two. Now some guys will shoot a dog that runs rabbits, but my friend was too kind hearted for that.

"About the middle of the day, the farmer stopped by to see how we were doin', and we told him our troubles.

'Well, said the farmer, Why don't you take Elmo here? He can point birds better than any dog you ever saw.'

"We looked around, but we didn't see any dog. We brought the fact to his attention.

'Not a dog,' says the farmer. 'My brother, Elmo.'

"Well, Elmo was a pretty simple lookin' feller, and we had our doubts, but we couldn't really turn down the offer. But it turned out Elmo was great! He could find a bird faster'n a preacher can spot counterfeit in the collection plate. I think my friend's dog learned a lot from him. Elmo always stayed in gun range, and he held his point solid as a statue. There's no doubt he was the best retriever I ever saw. We got our limit that day and the next. We made plans to come back next year.

Tom was taking this all in, but he hadn't just fallen off the tater truck, so naturally he was a little suspicious. "I take it you went back the next year?"

"We sure did," Pete said with a shake of his head, "but that farmer was upset with us when we asked to borrow Elmo."

Elmo isn't around anymore, he said.

You mean ... you don't mean he's dead? I asked.

Yes, and I think it's your fault, the farmer replied.

"I was downright shocked. *How can it be my fault?* I wanted to know.

After hangin' around that dog of yours, he developed bad habits, the farmer said.

You don't mean ...

Yep, says the farmer, *He took to runnin' rabbits an' we had to shoot him.*

I don't know what to think of today's politicians. It used to be that when you bought one, he stayed bought.

Have you ever tried putting liquid wax on your floor with a long handled paint roller? While we're on the subject of wax, you might like to try using car wax in your shower. It keeps the walls looking shiny clean and helps prevent mildew.

I'm not much of a drinker, but back when I was young and dumb, I maintained a good amateur standing. Like a lot of young fools, I thought drinking made you a man, when it really does just the opposite. Of course, people looked on drinking a lot different now than they used to. Back when the west was young, some of the women and darn near all of the men looked on drinking as the only year around sport. Well, almost the only year around sport. Anyhow, booze was made and sold just about everywhere, and it was looked on as a medicinal as well as recreational beverage. By the way, did you know that some of those old patent medicines ran about a hundred and twenty proof?

When prohibition came in, the whiskey makers just moved out into the brush and went to manufacturing their wet goods by the light of the moon. I'll bet you could still buy a quart of moonshine around here if you knew who to ask. It's usually sold in quart fruit jars and looks just like water. Believe me, it's not.

My dad made a little moon from time to time, and my grandad was a real professional. He always claimed he had it tougher than other moonshiners because his being a deputy sheriff made it tough to sell the product.

Anyhow, I came on the two of them down at the barn one evening, and they had a fruit jar with them. I was young and thought I was pretty tough. I'd forgotten that those two both had calluses on their noses from the rims of fruit jars rubbin' against 'em. Now, I'd drunk whiskey before, but never 'moon,' so I didn't take a real big swig when they offered me the jar. It was just as well. I could feel my teeth turning to chalk, and my mouth starting to burn, but I couldn't spit it out with them standing there grinning at me. I swallowed.

I'm telling you right now there isn't a car in America that couldn't get thirty miles per gallon on that stuff. I felt like an old muzzleloading rifle being cleaned with a barbed wire ramrod lubricated with gasoline. Those two may have been card carrying members of alcoholics unanimous, but one jolt of that stuff convinced me I'd never be in their league, and I'd better find another way to spend my time.

I was watching television the other night and saw some natives in a jungle somewhere wearing designer T-shirts and tennis shoes. Once headhunters and cannibals, these people were now drinking their tea with sugar (or their sugar with tea, depending on how you look at it) and using silverware. However, the narrator informed me that it was suspected that these folks still slipped off when no one was looking to engage in their former hobby. Well, that's civilization for you, and I guess that was the purpose of the program: to show how those people are like us — or how we're like them.

Martha and I have been married thirty-five years, and the thought of divorce has never crossed my mind. Murder has, but never divorce.

I went to the doctor the other day, and I'm not too sure about him. He's pretty young, but at least he's got sense enough to admit he doesn't know everything — which puts him a couple jumps ahead of most of the doctors I've met.

My last doctor was a fella about my age. He kept telling me all about the things I shouldn't do, like smoke or drink or eat fatty foods. When he got tired of that, he'd tell me all the things I should be doing. For example, he exercised everyday, ate right and didn't drink or smoke. In other words, I should be more like him. I guess he was right. People must have admired him for his clean living, because there were sure a lot of 'em showed up at his funeral.

So, anyhow, I go to see this young doctor and tell him I've been feeling a little run down lately. He tells me he can't make me young again. What a revelation. I told him that wasn't what I had in mind. I'd just like to go on getting older.

I've got a real problem when I go to vote these days. Sometimes I don't know either candidate. That makes it a tough decision. Sometimes I do know the candidates. That makes it a tougher decision. Well, that's what makes democracy such a fine thing. We get to choose who robs us.

We used to trail our cattle up into the Blue Mountains in the spring. They'd graze up there all summer, and we'd bring them down in the fall. Once we got them rounded up, we'd have them back on the home place in a couple of days. That was because in the fall, we didn't have any little calves along.

In the spring it was different. The calves that were born before or during the drive would be hauled along in the back of a truck with their anxious mommas following along behind. We'd work on those calves before we turned the cows loose for the summer. That is, we would earmark them, give them their shots, and castrate the bull calves.

The late calves, those that were born after the cattle were turned loose, were a problem. A couple of riders would check periodically, looking for new calves. Sam Johnson and I worked that job together one year.

First, you have to understand that a kid with a good horse and a rope thinks he's just about the greatest invention since sliced bread. After he develops a little skill, he'd rope an elephant if one happened by.

Well, one didn't happen by ... but a cow elk and her calf did. I'd just busted through some brush, coming up out of a canyon that was steep as a mule's face when I saw them. I tickled old Smokey with the spurs and dropped a loop over that calf elk as slick as a whistle. I was about to turn him loose when Sam rode up.

"Wait a minute," he said. "Since you've got him caught, we may as well do things right."

A couple of years later, I was in the Army. When I got my discharge, I spent two years in college. Then Martha and I got married. A year or so later, the kids started coming along, and I kept looking for work that paid better to feed my growing family. I was working as a sheet metal man when I first heard an odd story.

A lot of the guys who worked there were hunters, and there was a story that kept making the rounds about a huge bull elk that was roaming the Blue Mountains. Not only was he a giant, but he was also smart. Very few people had seen him, and most of them only got a glimpse. But it was agreed by all that he was a monster, and that he was smarter and more cautious of men than any elk in the country.

Well, the years passed, and I was working as a meatcutter when someone finally brought him

down. A wondrous thing was discovered about that elk. He had no, shall we say, reproductive capability. In other words, he was a steer elk. His picture and that of the hunter was in all the local papers. It was theorized by many experts that this oddity of nature had contributed to the animal's exceptionally long life since he didn't engage in the rut, or mating season, each fall, and therefore went into the winter months in prime condition. Personally, I think the only reason anybody ever got him is that he was so old that he'd become senile, or maybe he took the easy way out. They said his teeth were all worn off, and if that was true, then Ma Nature was sure to take a hand. Just between us, if I've gotta go, I'd rather be shot than starve to death.

Anyhow, this hunter had him stuffed, and it was a fine head. It made the record books easily. The only thing that looked a little odd were those ears, but the experts said he must have split them on a snag of limb or got in a fight with another elk sometime over the years.

Well, I kept waiting for old Sam to come clean, but he never did. He died a few years back and is probably sitting up there on a cloud chuckling at this very minute.

It's been so long now that I don't recall the name of the hunter, but I think if he reads this, he'll know who he is and finally know how this all came to pass.

For my part, I just think Sam and I deserve a place in the record book along with that hunter. I won't even ask for my elk back. My elk? Well, of course, it is ... it's got my earmark on it.

I hear that Elmer walked into the tavern one day and asked Jensen, "What d'you got for a headache?"

"Well, gee," Jensen said, as he looked around, "I don't think I've got any aspirin or anything ..."

"You don't understand," replied Elmer, "I don't want to get rid of one ... I want to get one."

Martha is always talking about "women's intuition." Well that may be, but I think a good part of the time she mistakes intuition for plain ol' suspicion.

You know you're getting old when you don't care where your wife goes so long as she doesn't drag you along with her.

When the kids were little we were getting ready to go to Martha's folks for Thanksgiving dinner. I went out to warm up the car and it wouldn't start. The boys watched me for a while and then went back in the house.

Martha was finishing putting on her makeup when the boys walked in.

"The car is busted," Curt announced.

"Oh, no," Martha said. "did Daddy say he could fix it?"

"You want me to leave out the bad words?"

"Yes."

"He didn't say."

Most folks around here remember old Herman Snipes. He was about as ornery and hard-to-get-along-with as anybody I ever met. Now you may think I'm being hard on old Herman, but the fact is that when he fell in the river and drowned, they found the body seven miles upstream.

Pete was telling us about a little fishing trip he took a few years ago. It seems he got up early, ate a bite of breakfast, threw his stuff in the pickup and took off. He was almost to the river when he realized he'd forgotten the lunch Gladys had packed for him the night before. Since he planned to spend the day, he wanted that lunch, so he turned around and headed home, upset with himself about forgetting it.

He'd only gone a mile or so when he saw the hitchhiker. Pete had seen him earlier, but the guy was headed the other way, so Pete had paid him no mind. Now, with the sun coming up, Pete knew he'd be getting a late start anyway, so he stopped and picked this fella up.

They were driving along and Pete was squinting into the rising sun as they talked. This fella seemed kind of restless and moved around in the seat quite a lot, but Pete thought he was just settling in. After all, it was still eight or ten miles back to town.

Pete was feeling a little low. There had been plenty of gas in the tank to make the trip when he'd left that morning, but now, with the extra driving he'd have to stop and get more. Pete's fishing vest was there on the seat beside him, and he always kept his wallet in a zippered pocket of that vest when he went fishing. There was less chance of it getting wet. Pete reached for the vest and found the pocket, but it was unzipped and the wallet was gone.

The hitchhiker was talking about where he had been and where he was headed. It seems he was one of those fellas who followed the harvests, and he said he only worked long enough to buy his booze and some party time with whatever loose women were available before moving on.

Now you have to understand that Pete's a little sudden. He keeps an old forty-four caliber hog leg under the seat of his pickup, and he knows how to use it. In his younger days, Pete was in quite a few fist fights. He was known to fight at the drop of a hat and, if necessary, drop the hat himself. Just now, old Pete was really scorched. He pulled over. The hitchhiker was still talking when Pete reached under the seat, jerked out his old six-shooter, and shoved about an inch of the barrel up this fella's nose.

"Hand over the wallet," hissed Pete, as he

eared back the hammer.

The bum's eyes were about as big as a couple of bongo drums, and he didn't waste any time doing as he was told.

Pete reached across him and opened the door. "Now, get out," Pete yelled, as he pushed the guy onto the pavement. "You're lucky I don't just stop your clock right here."

Pete drove off, and he was still fuming when he got to the house.

Gladys met him at the door. "It's a good thing you came back," she said.

"Yeah, I know. I forgot my lunch. Listen," Pete went on, "you'll never guess ..."

"Yes, and you forgot your wallet, too," said Gladys.

Pete doesn't pick up hitchhikers anymore. He says it's too dangerous. I can see where it would be.

A bird in the hand is worth two in the bush. Maybe, but I wouldn't look underneath that bird if I were you.

Golf is kind of a funny game. It's about all that men talk about around the office. Then they finally get out on the golf course, and all they talk about is business.

When I first saw him, he scared me half to death. He had long, shaggy black hair, a big triangular head and a mouthful of the longest, sharpest looking teeth I'd ever seen on a dog. He was as tall as Cathy, our three-year-old, and she was standing there feeding him dog food she'd filched from the sack we kept for Sam.

He must have weighed a hundred and twenty or thirty pounds. He could have swallowed my daughter in one gulp. I reached behind the door and picked up the rifle we kept there. "Cathy," I said, "come here." She didn't hear me and kept right on petting this monster while I chambered a cartridge. The dog looked toward me, his pointed ears erect atop his big, ugly head. There was nothing of a normal dog in that look. There was no joy, certainly no fear, and the only impression I had was one of pure, savage power and the willingness to use it on anything that got in his way.

The dog turned and walked away into the trees. I would have shot him right then if Cathy hadn't been between us. My daughter scampered to my side and pointed into the woods. "Nice doggy, Daddy."

I breathed a sigh of relief and looked down at Sam, our cow dog. Sam wasn't afraid of anything that wore hair, and he'd tackle a two thousand pound bull in a flash. He didn't permit other dogs in his territory. And yet he had sat there, watching all this and never made a sound. I couldn't understand why.

A horse had fallen with my Dad, and he was still pretty stoved up when it came branding time. I took a vacation from my job as a police officer and came out to help. Martha and the kids came with me.

That evening I saw Cathy taking a pie plate heaped with dog food out to the edge of the woods. I saw it and I didn't do anything, maybe because Sam didn't. In a minute that huge dog appeared from the woods and ate the food while Cathy petted him. It went on that way for a week.

The corral was a big square pen made of two-by-six boards with old railroad ties for posts. Right down the middle was a runway or alley that was maybe ten feet wide at one side that narrowed down to a squeeze chute at the other. This was fine for working with cows, but it was too big for the calves. There was one big enclosure on the north side of the alley and two smaller ones to the south. We worked on the calves in there. The wide end of the alley was left open, because we weren't using it. The cows were outside the corral bawling for their calves.

When we finished with a calf, we'd push him through one of the small gates on that side. His mother would rush up to him, make sure he was okay and then they'd wander off. Those old range cows are nothing to fool with, and some of them will fight to protect their young. There was one in particular in that bunch who would charge a man afoot whether she had a calf or not. She was still hanging around, so I knew we still had her calf in the corral.

We were working on a calf when I noticed this ornery cow had come through the open gate and up the alley. I didn't think much about it, because there was still a fence between us. Then I heard her horns scraping wood. At that point she barely had enough room to turn around. I glanced over to see what she was looking at and saw Cathy standing in the alley.

You wonder how kids do it. Martha said she was right there in the kitchen one minute and the next she was gone. Cathy had come down to the corral, crawled under the fence and crossed the big pen. Then she crawled under the next fence and into the alleyway. That killer range cow was between me and my daughter.

The cow started for her, and there was nothing I could do. It was like seeing your kid standing on the railroad tracks as a locomotive roars down on her. Cathy was standing there with her big blue eyes wide, and I was so scared all I could do was scream her name.

I don't know where he came from. It just seemed like a big, black shadow passed over Cathy's head and that dog was there. It was narrow in the alley, and there was no place to turn, no way to avoid that charge. But then he had no intention of turning. He came straight ahead, and he came hard and fast.

Just as they met, he gave a savage growl and drove himself at her head. He slowed her down, but she hooked him and knocked him back and sideways into the fence. He went down, but he scrambled to his feet, snarling and growling so loud it seems I can hear it yet. Those big teeth of his were doing their job, and I saw hair flying as she got another horn into him and drove him back into the boards. I've never seen such savagery; I've never seen such heart. He fought back with everything he had, knowing he couldn't last much longer, but knowing too that he was all there was between a little girl and death. With a horn in his chest, he pushed it in further, driving forward to sink his teeth into the cow's neck. Slowly, then faster, he drove her back.

And then it was over. The cow turned and rushed up the alley bleeding from a dozen deep wounds. Somehow I had climbed the fence and dropped into the alley. I had to climb up again to let her go by.

I ran toward my daughter, and the big dog standing beside her. Cathy extended her arms toward me, and I scooped her up, hugging her to my chest for a long minute. Then I looked down at that big, bloody head at my side and put my hand gently on it.

"I was wrong about you," I said.

Slowly the big dog sank to the ground. I kneeled beside him and stroked his head and muzzle.

"I owe you one, pardner. I owe you."

He licked my hand ... and died.

We buried him there at the edge of the woods where Cathy used to feed him. I made a little wooden marker and placed it there. It was kind of flimsy, and I knew I'd need to replace it in a year or so. At the time I thought I'd have one done in stone, and maybe I will someday if the ranch should pass from the family's hands. But for now, I'll just do what I've always done. I'll make up a new marker each year to replace the old one, but the words I carve in it are always the same.

PARDNER
I.O.U.

There are some debts you can never repay ... you can only keep up the interest.

Say now, we're sure glad you dropped in. Sure, you have to be on your way, but don't forget the way back, okay? We'll be lookin' for you.

AUTHOR'S NOTE

Ever since I can remember, I've enjoyed talking to the old timers. They're just waiting to tell someone the stories of their youth, or the tales passed down by their parents and grandparents. If I talk to enough of them, I'm sure to hear a story now and again that is very much like one I've heard before. The people involved may change, or the circumstances might be somewhat different — even the punch line (if there is one) may be altered to some degree, but it's the same story. That's fine with me. There's always something different, even in a story I've heard before. Sauce, as they say, for the goose.

For example, there's the story of the time when the Army mechanized all its units and some animals were simply turned loose to wander away. A neophyte hunter went looking for a deer not long after that and bagged a big one. At the checkout station he couldn't wait to show the game officer the huge "mule deer" he'd taken. Naturally, the critter had long ears, shoes on its hooves, and a "U.S." branded on it. I've heard half a dozen people swear it happened right in their area.

The old timers have something to tell you. If you're not fortunate enough to have one in the family, or close at hand, then stop in at a nearby retirement home. Spend an hour a week if you can, but an hour a month or even an hour a year is something. And, believe me, you'll both be better for it.

GDT